30+ Fractal Artworks

ADULT COLORING BOOK

VOL. 2

COLOR TESTING

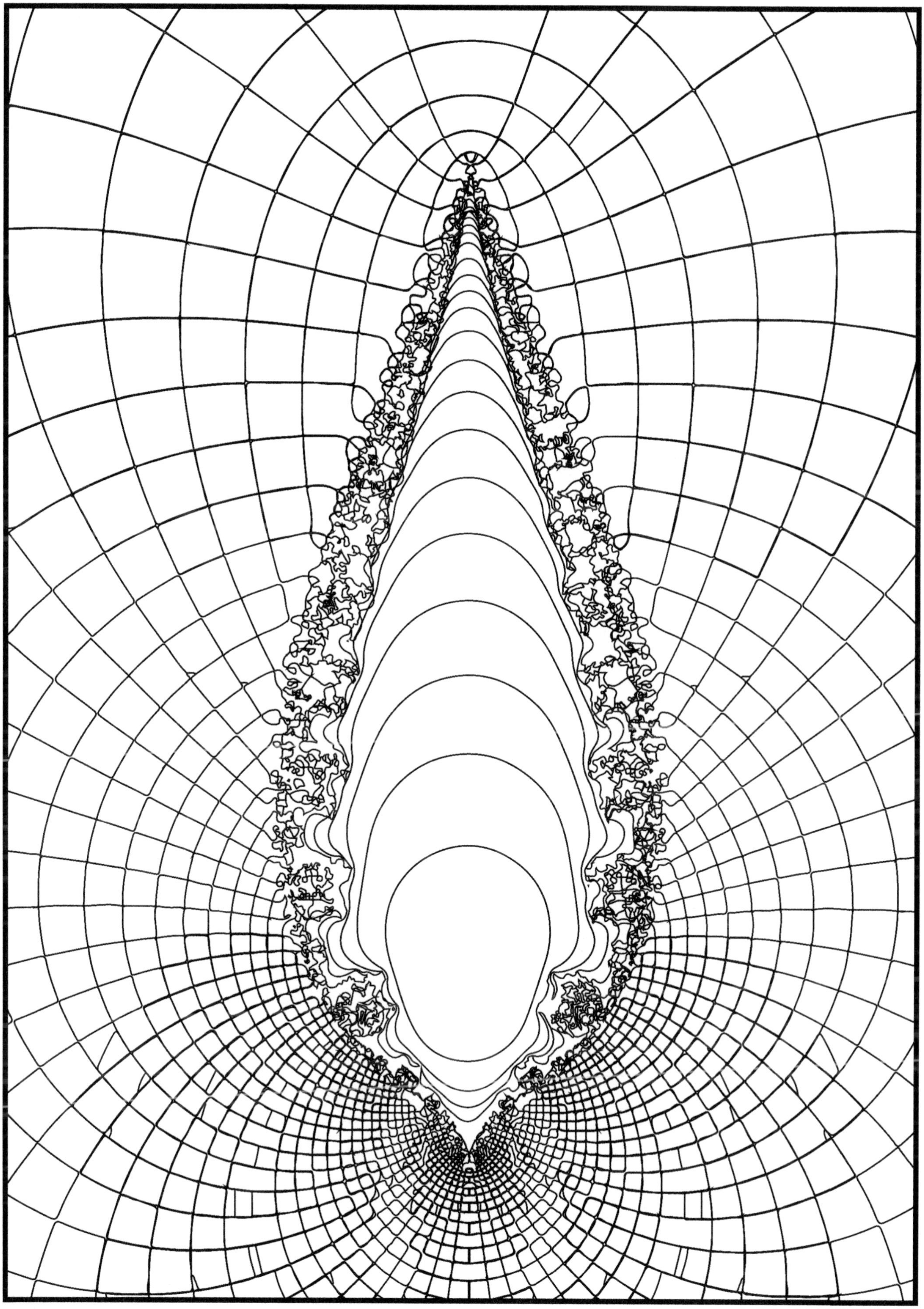

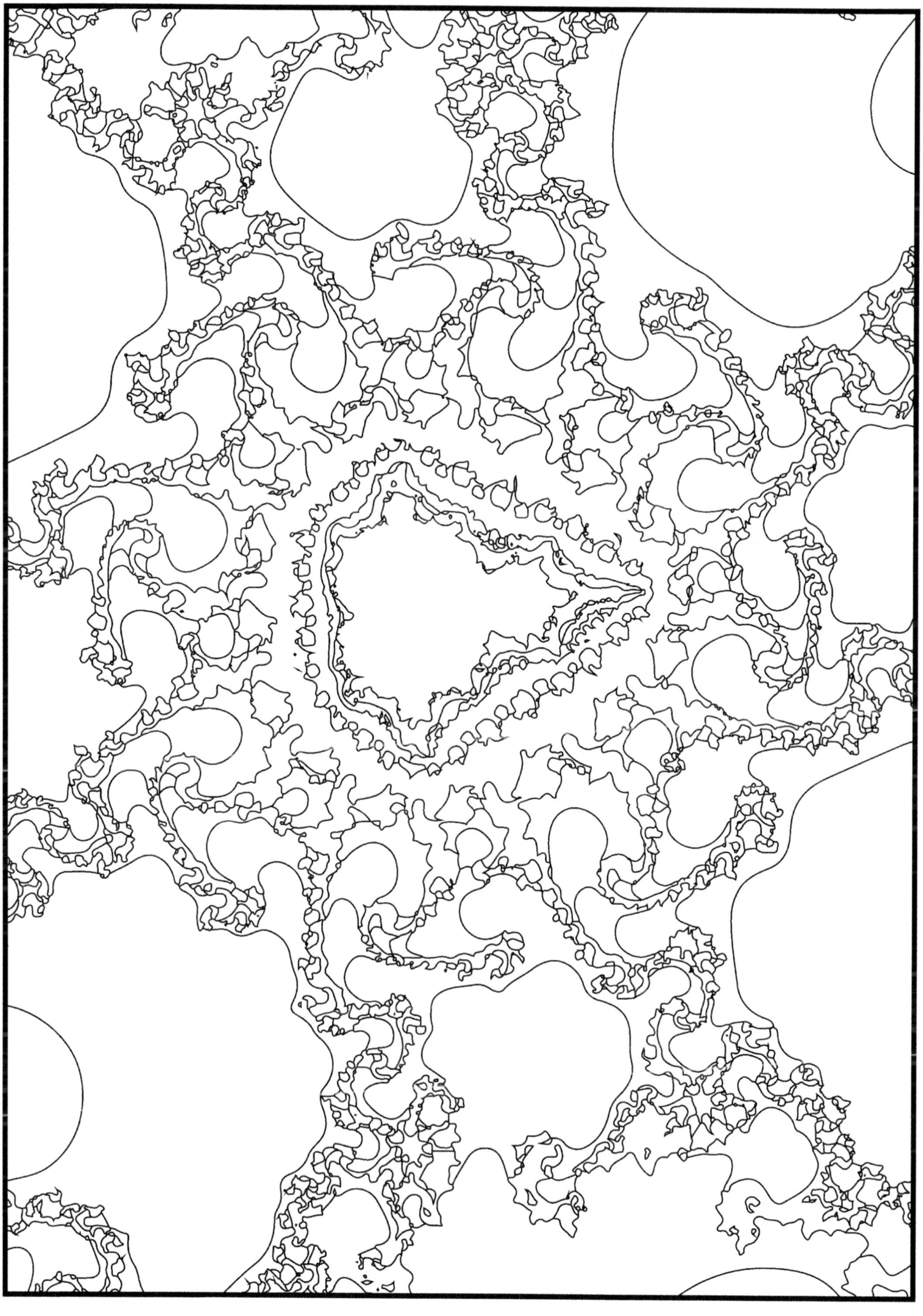

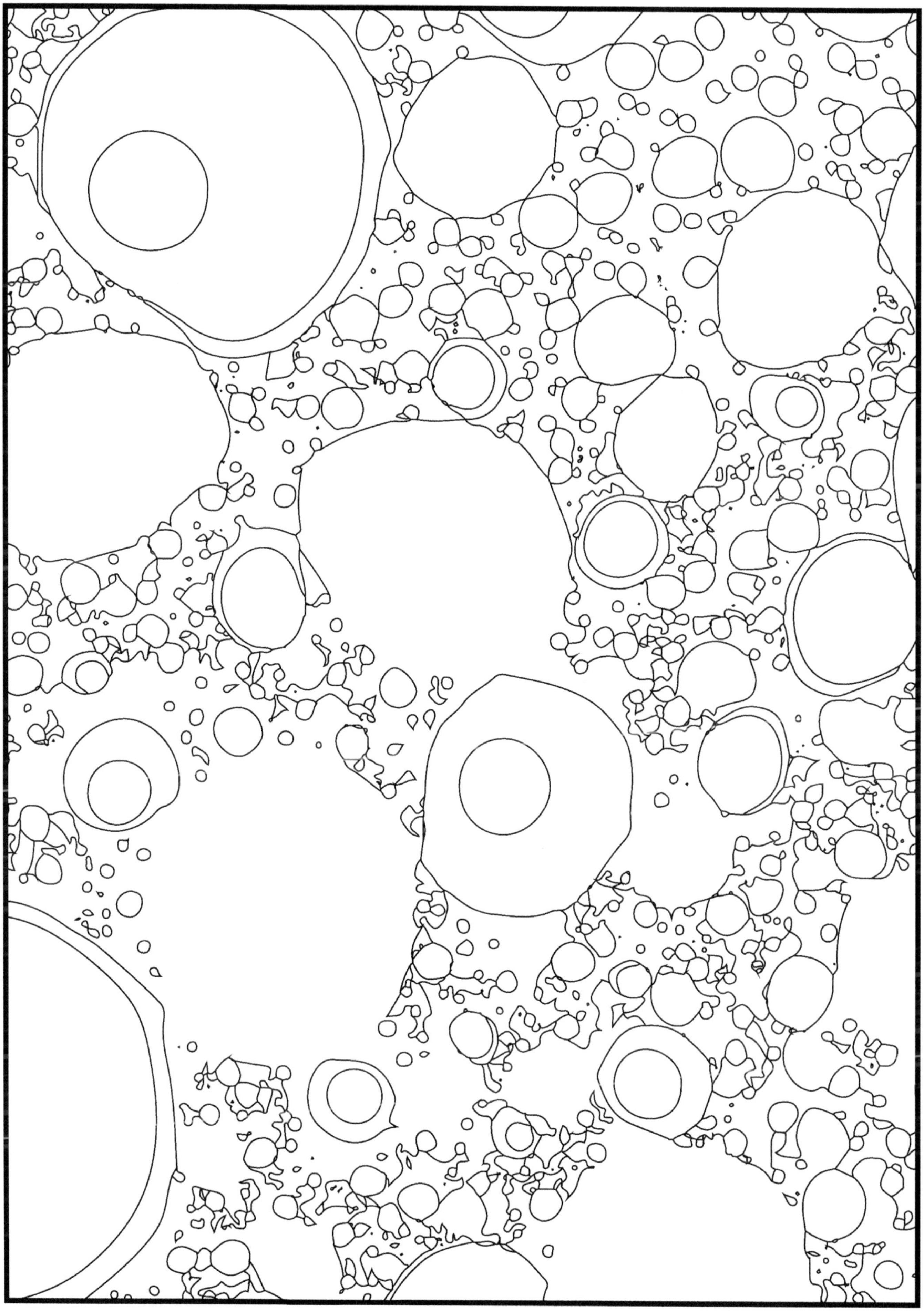

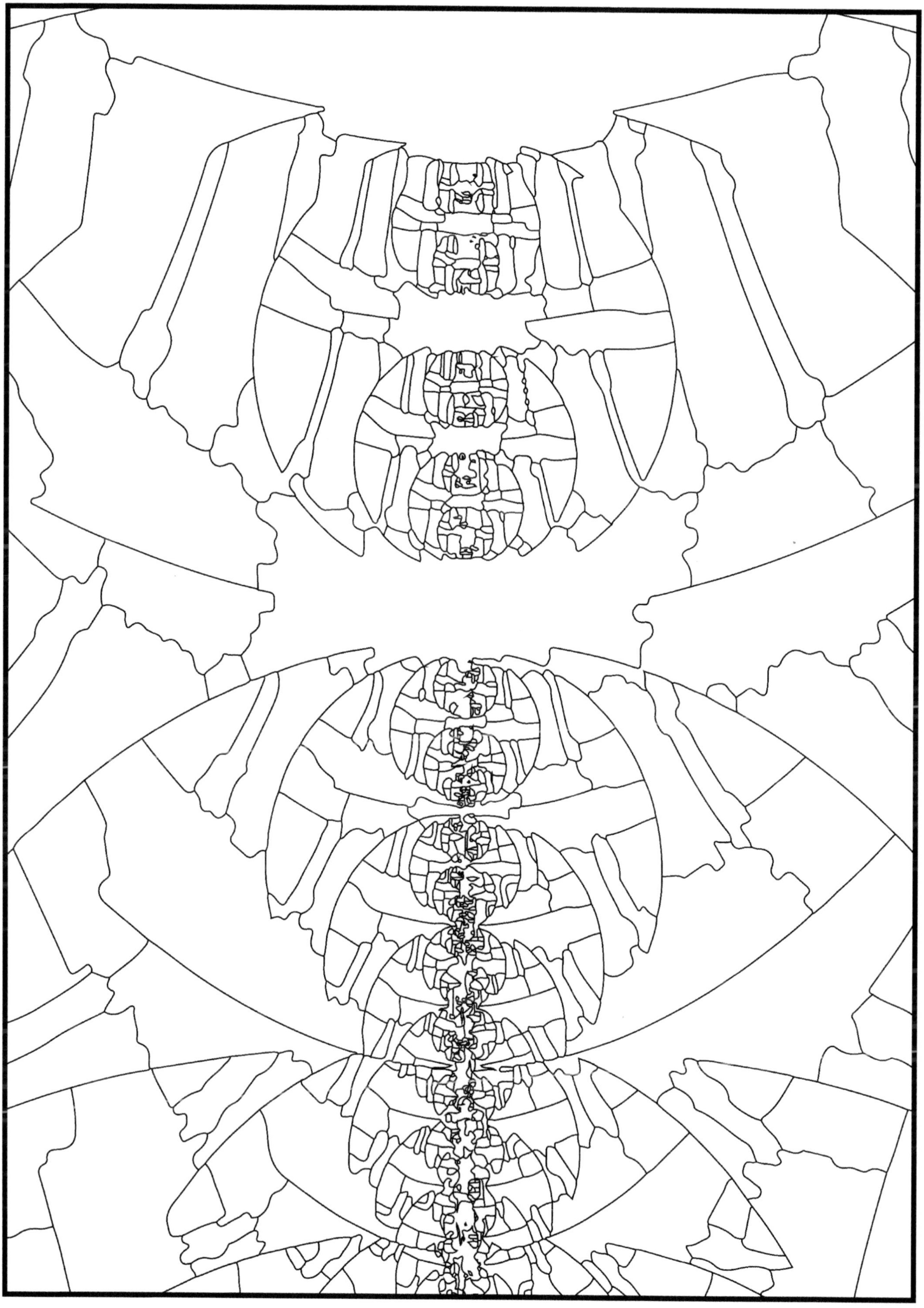

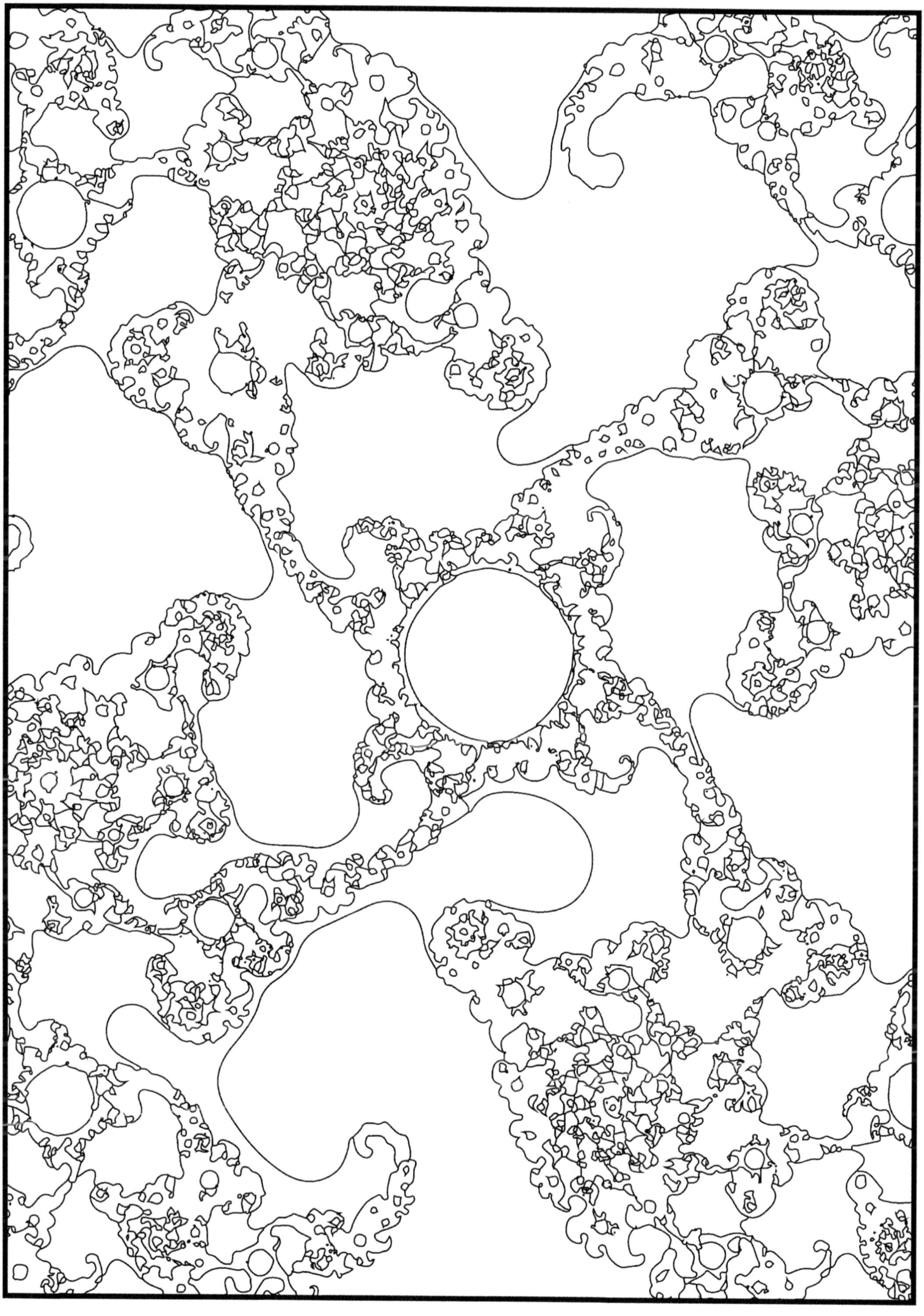

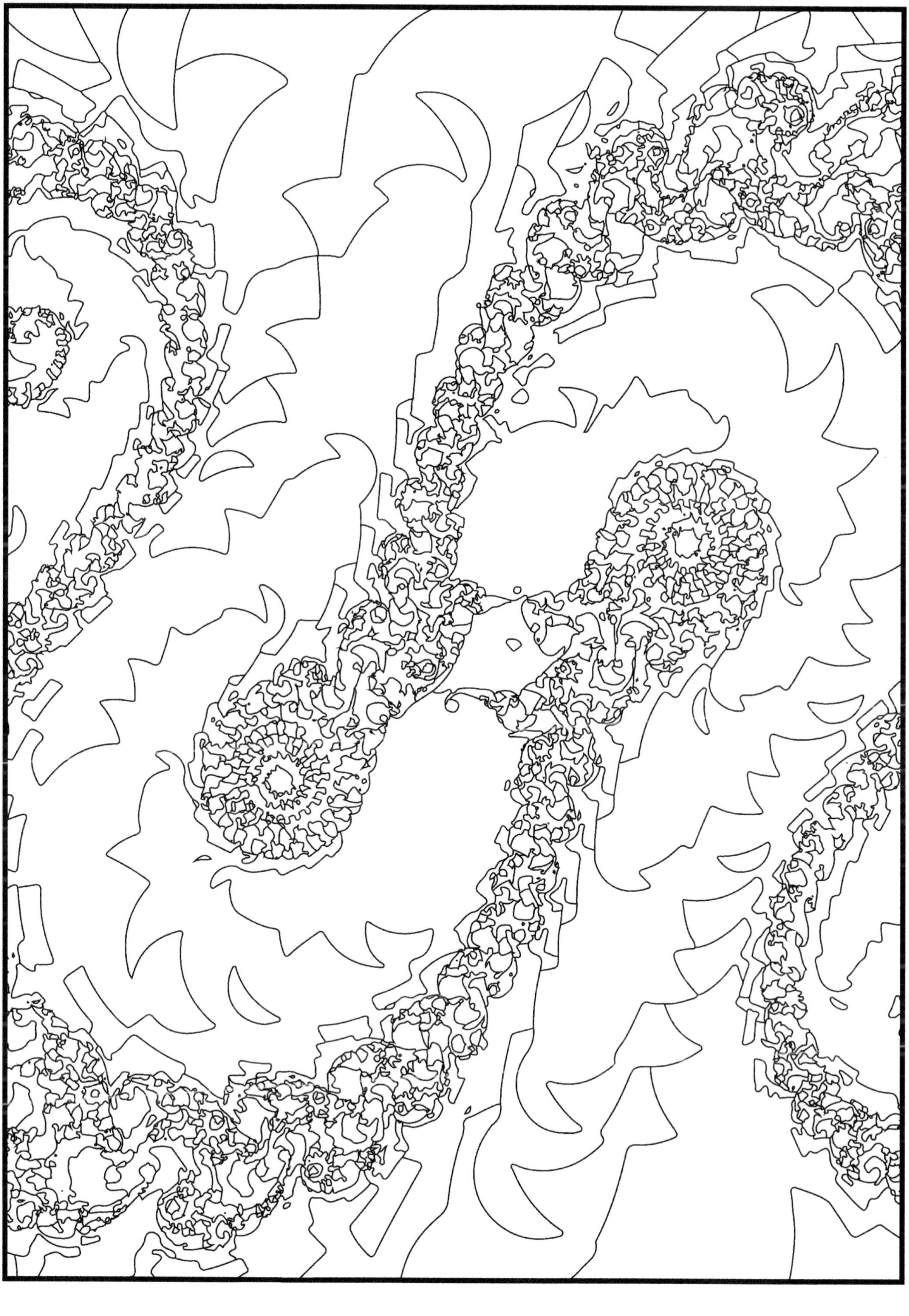

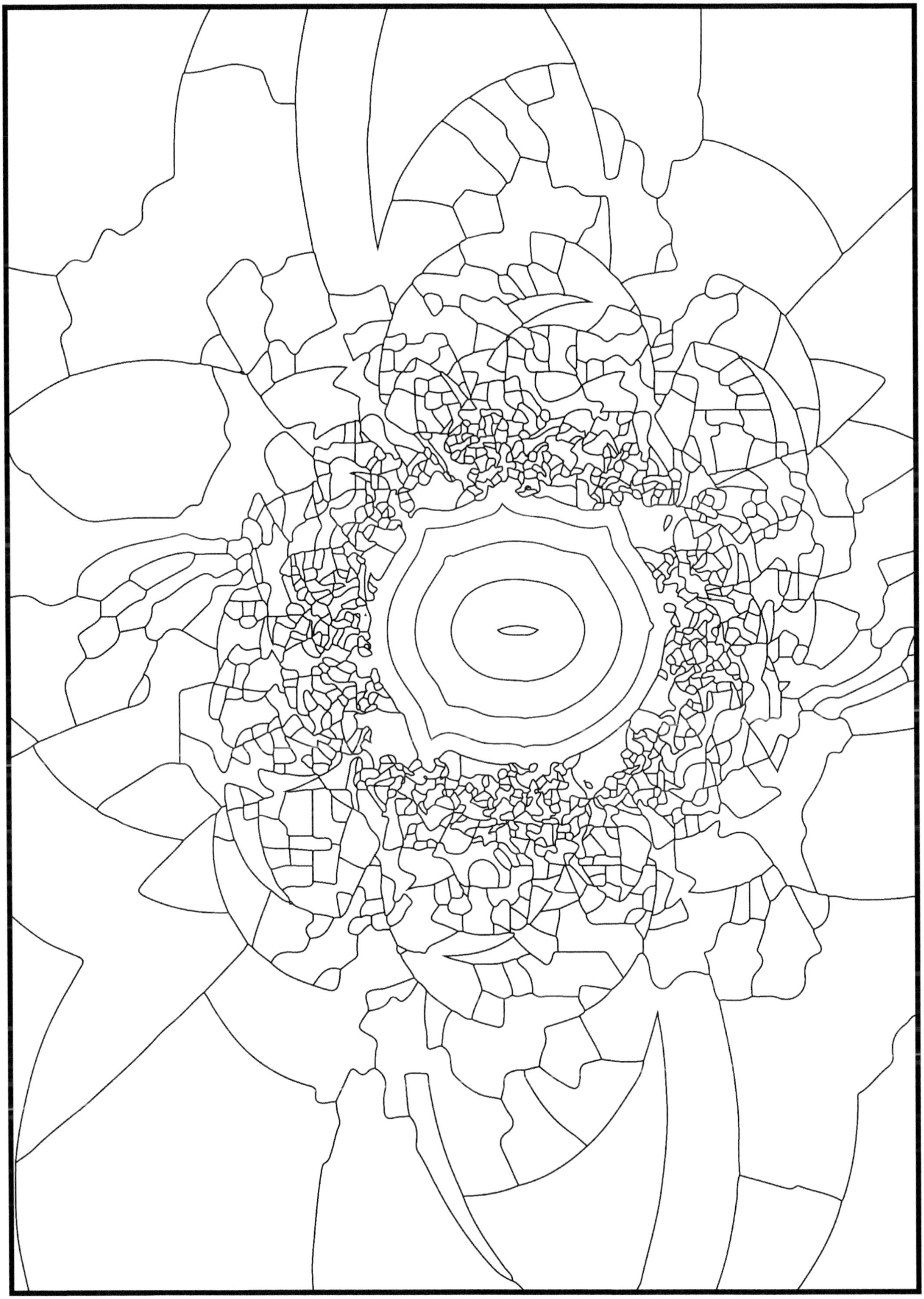

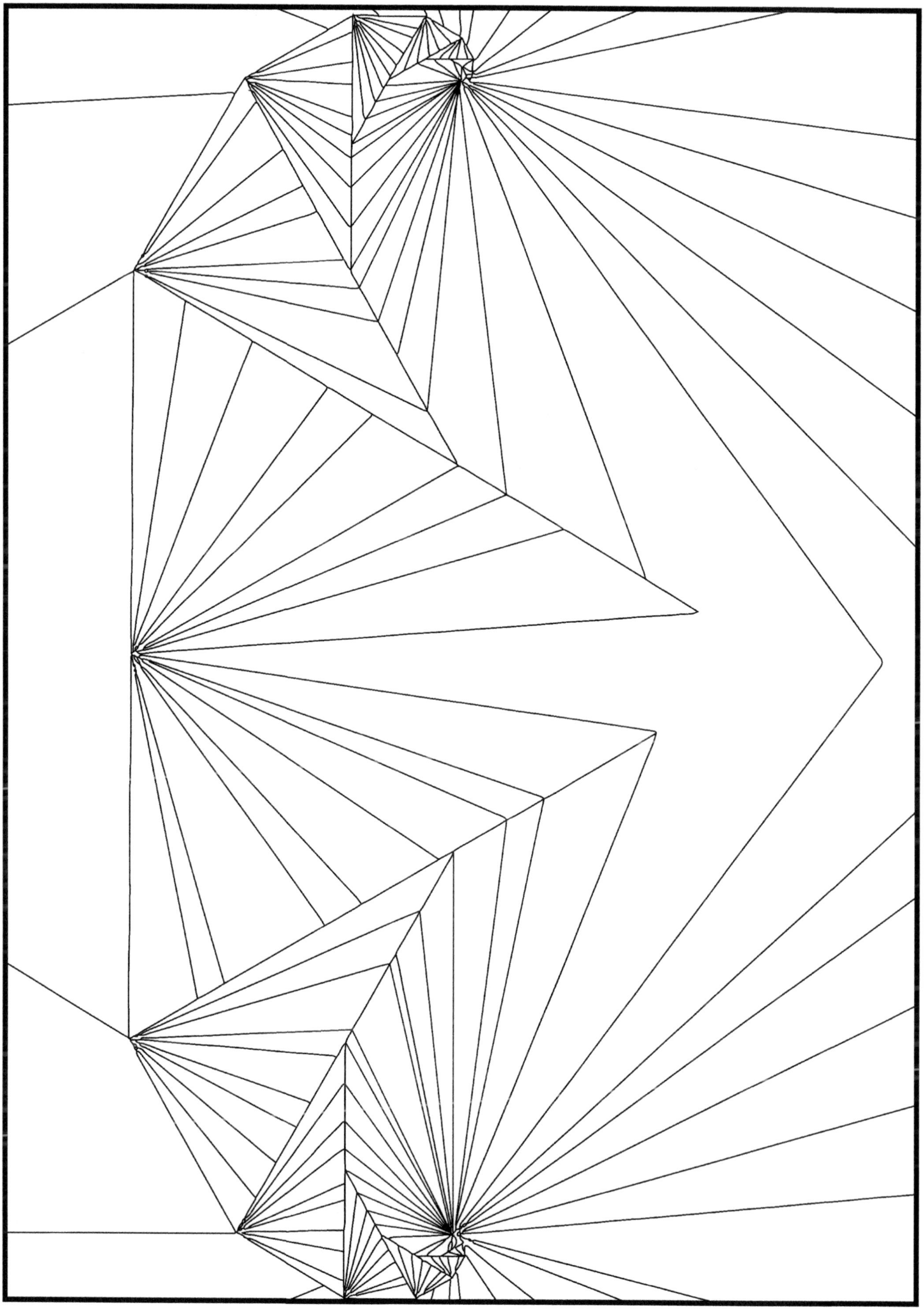

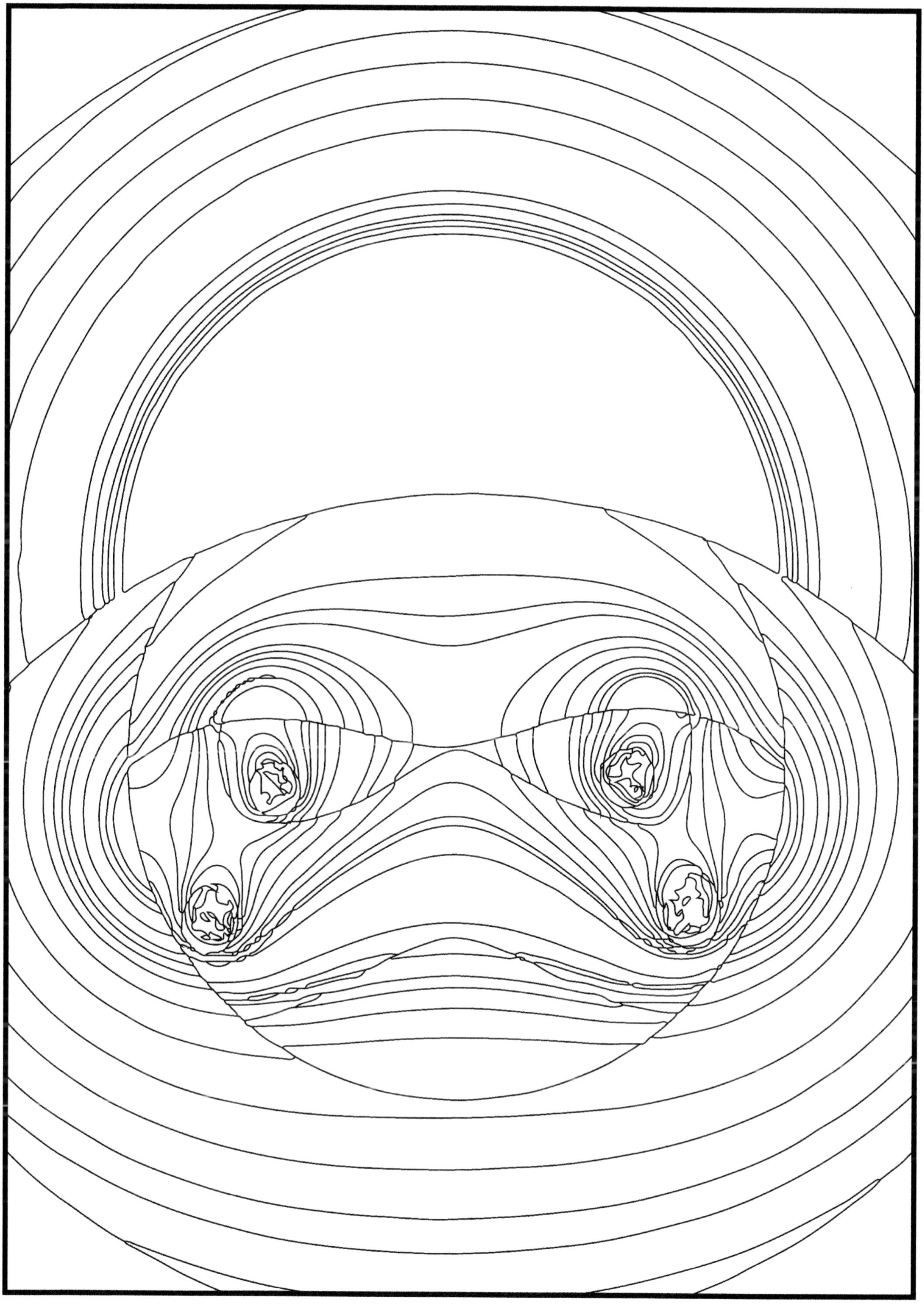

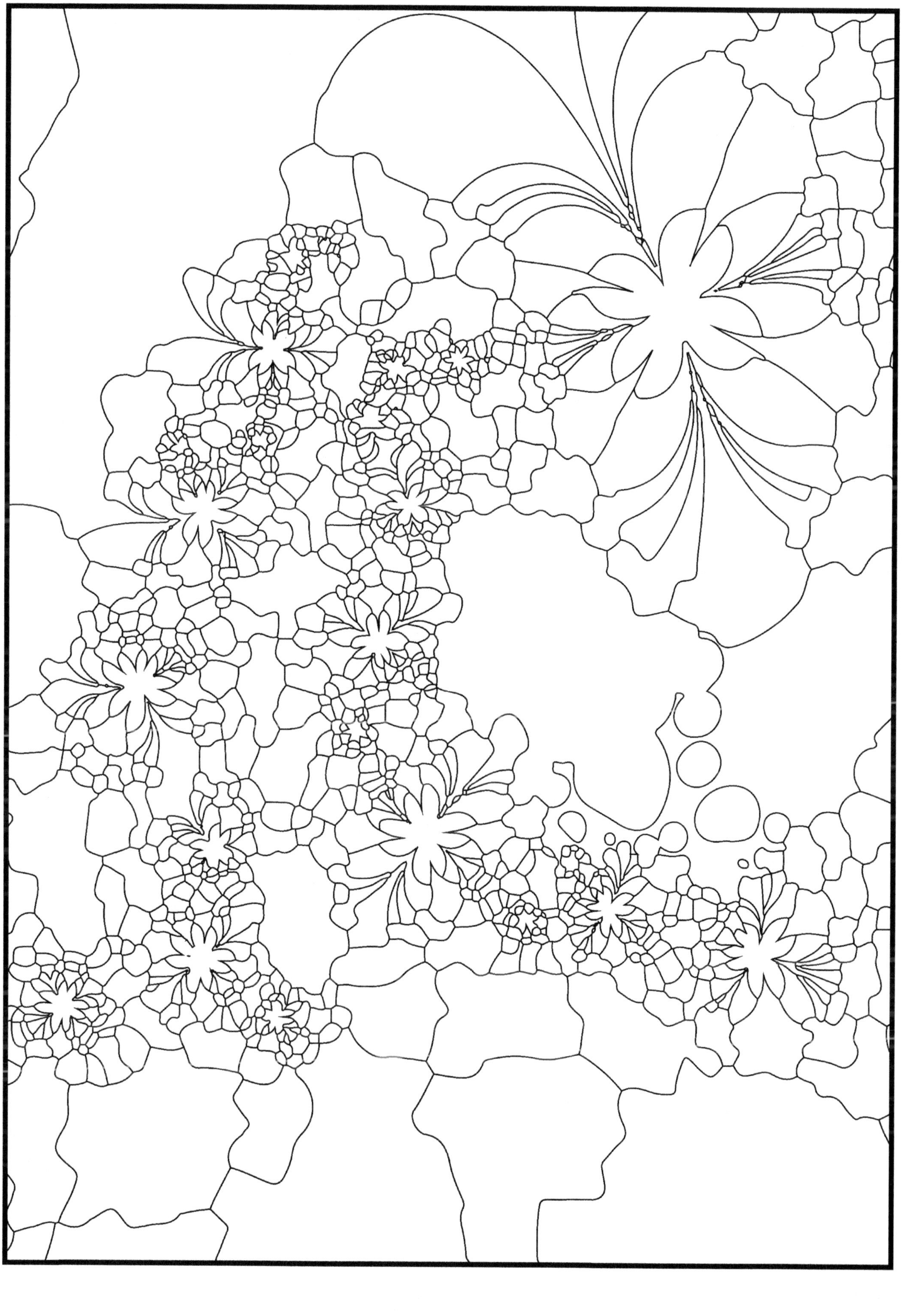

Printed in Great Britain
by Amazon

81219947R00045